AI in Healthcare

Revolutionizing Patient Care with Artificial Intelligence

Carl Keyness

TABLE OF CONTENTS

Chapter 1: Introduction to AI in Healthcare

In the rapidly evolving landscape of healthcare, artificial intelligence (AI) is emerging as a transformative force, revolutionizing patient care from diagnosis to treatment. This chapter serves as the gateway to our exploration of AI's impact on healthcare by providing an in-depth understanding of the evolution of healthcare technology, the pivotal role of AI in modern healthcare, and an overview of the book's contents.

The Evolution of Healthcare Technology

Healthcare has long been a domain characterized by innovation and technological advancements. The journey of healthcare technology has been marked by significant milestones that have continually improved patient care and medical practices. Over the years, we have witnessed the transformation of healthcare technology in the following key ways:

Early Medical Instruments: The roots of healthcare technology can be traced back to the development of early medical instruments, such as the stethoscope and thermometer. These inventions marked the beginning of medical precision and diagnostic accuracy.

Radiology and Imaging: The advent of X-ray technology revolutionized medical imaging, allowing physicians to visualize the internal structures of the human body. This breakthrough greatly enhanced the ability to diagnose and treat various medical conditions.

Electronic Health Records (EHRs): The digitalization of health records and the implementation of EHRs have streamlined patient information management. EHRs have improved data accessibility, reducing errors and enhancing patient care.

Telemedicine: The concept of telemedicine has made healthcare accessible to remote and underserved areas. Telehealth technologies enable remote consultations, diagnosis, and treatment, extending medical services to a broader population.

Genomic Medicine: Advances in genomics and personalized medicine have allowed for tailored treatment plans based on an individual's genetic makeup. This has opened new possibilities for targeted therapies and disease prevention.

Wearable Devices: The proliferation of wearable devices, such as fitness trackers and smartwatches, has empowered individuals to take control of their health. These devices monitor vital signs and collect health data for better self-management.

Big Data and Analytics: The accumulation of vast amounts of healthcare data has given rise to the application of big data analytics in healthcare. Data-driven insights have improved patient outcomes and enhanced medical research.

The integration of artificial intelligence represents the latest and most transformative phase in the evolution of healthcare technology. AI's ability to analyze vast datasets, interpret complex medical images, and facilitate personalized care has opened up a new era in healthcare innovation.

The Role of AI in Modern Healthcare

Artificial intelligence has rapidly gained prominence in modern healthcare due to its capacity to address some of the most pressing challenges in the field. Its role is multifaceted and encompasses the following key aspects:

Diagnostic Precision: AI-driven algorithms can analyze medical images and data with unparalleled precision, aiding in early disease detection and accurate diagnosis.

Personalized Treatment: AI can customize treatment plans based on a patient's unique genetic, clinical, and lifestyle data, enhancing the effectiveness of therapies.

Efficiency and Automation: AI automates administrative tasks, reducing the burden on healthcare professionals and streamlining healthcare operations.

Predictive Analytics: AI's predictive capabilities help healthcare providers anticipate patient needs, allowing for proactive interventions and improved patient outcomes.

Remote Patient Monitoring: AI facilitates remote patient monitoring, enabling real-time tracking of vital signs and patient conditions, enhancing patient care, and reducing readmissions.

Drug Discovery: AI accelerates drug discovery processes, enabling the development of new therapies and medications at a faster pace.

Robotic Surgery: AI-powered surgical robots provide precision and minimally invasive surgical options, reducing patient recovery times and complications.

Natural Language Processing: AI-driven NLP enables efficient clinical documentation and assists in extracting valuable insights from medical records.

Overview of the Book

This book delves deep into the realm of AI in healthcare, exploring the multifaceted ways in which artificial intelligence is transforming patient care. Throughout the chapters, we will unravel the applications of AI in disease diagnosis, personalized treatment, medical imaging, remote patient monitoring, drug discovery, and more. We will also address the ethical and legal considerations surrounding the use of AI in healthcare, as well as examine the future of healthcare as we embark on a journey into uncharted territories.

The chapters that follow will provide insights, case studies, and examples of AI's positive impact on healthcare, showcasing the incredible potential of AI to revolutionize patient care and medical practices. Whether you are a healthcare professional, a patient, or simply curious about the future of healthcare, this book will illuminate the path toward a new era in patient care—driven by the power of artificial intelligence.

Chapter 2: Understanding Artificial Intelligence in Healthcare

Artificial Intelligence (AI) is not only revolutionizing the healthcare industry, but it is also reshaping the way we diagnose, treat, and care for patients. In this chapter, we will explore the fundamentals of AI in healthcare, including what AI is, its various types, and the critical ethical and regulatory considerations that govern its use.

What Is Artificial Intelligence in Healthcare?

Artificial Intelligence, often abbreviated as AI, refers to the simulation of human intelligence in machines that are programmed to think and learn like humans. In healthcare, AI takes on the role of assisting healthcare professionals and healthcare systems in tasks that typically require human intelligence. It can process, analyze, and interpret vast amounts of medical data with a speed and accuracy that surpass human capabilities.

AI in healthcare encompasses a wide range of applications, from medical imaging to drug discovery and patient care. Some of the key areas where AI has a significant impact include:

Disease Diagnosis: AI can assist in diagnosing various medical conditions by analyzing patient data, medical images, and genetic information. It aids in early disease detection and improves diagnostic accuracy.

Personalized Treatment: AI algorithms can develop personalized treatment plans based on an individual's medical history, genetics, and lifestyle factors. This ensures that treatments are tailored to the specific needs of each patient.

Medical Imaging: AI is highly effective in interpreting medical images, such as X-rays, MRIs, and CT scans. It can detect abnormalities, assist radiologists, and enhance diagnostic precision.

Drug Discovery: AI accelerates the drug discovery process by predicting potential drug candidates, identifying new molecular targets, and optimizing clinical trial designs.

Predictive Analytics: AI algorithms can predict disease outbreaks, patient outcomes, and healthcare resource needs. They enable proactive interventions and resource allocation.

Administrative Efficiency: AI streamlines administrative tasks in healthcare, reducing the burden on healthcare professionals and improving operational efficiency.

Natural Language Processing (NLP): NLP technology allows AI to interpret and extract insights from unstructured clinical notes and patient records, making it easier to access and utilize this valuable information.

Types of AI in Healthcare

In healthcare, AI can be categorized into several types, each serving specific purposes. Some common types of AI in healthcare include:

Machine Learning (ML): Machine learning is a subset of AI that focuses on training algorithms to learn from data and make predictions or decisions. In healthcare, ML is widely used for diagnostic purposes, predictive analytics, and personalized treatment plans.

Deep Learning: Deep learning is a subset of ML that involves neural networks with multiple layers. It is particularly effective in image and speech recognition tasks, making it invaluable for interpreting medical images.

Natural Language Processing (NLP): NLP enables AI systems to understand and interpret human language. In healthcare, NLP is used to extract valuable information from medical records, enabling better patient care and research.

Robotic Process Automation (RPA): RPA automates repetitive administrative tasks, reducing the workload on healthcare professionals and improving operational efficiency in healthcare institutions.

Predictive Analytics: Predictive analytics uses historical data to make predictions about future events. In healthcare, it is applied to forecast patient outcomes and resource requirements.

Computer Vision: Computer vision enables machines to interpret and analyze visual information. It is especially useful in medical imaging, as it can assist in the interpretation of X-rays, CT scans, and other medical images.

Ethical and Regulatory Considerations

The integration of AI in healthcare raises critical ethical and regulatory considerations that must be carefully addressed:

Privacy and Data Security: AI systems require access to sensitive patient data. Protecting patient privacy and ensuring robust data security measures are in place is of utmost importance.

Transparency and Explainability: AI algorithms often operate as black boxes, making it challenging to understand their decision-making processes. Ensuring transparency and explainability is essential to gain trust from healthcare professionals and patients.

Bias and Fairness: AI systems can inadvertently perpetuate biases present in training data. Careful monitoring and mitigation of bias is required to ensure that AI does not discriminate against certain patient groups.

Regulatory Compliance: Healthcare regulations and compliance standards must be adhered to when implementing AI systems in healthcare. Meeting these requirements ensures that AI is used safely and ethically.

Informed Consent: Patients should be informed about the use of AI in their healthcare and provide consent for its use in their treatment.

Professional Oversight: AI should be seen as a tool to assist healthcare professionals, not replace them. Human expertise and oversight are critical for the safety and quality of patient care.

In the chapters that follow, we will delve deeper into the specific applications of AI in healthcare, including AI's role in disease diagnosis, personalized treatment, medical imaging, drug discovery, and more. We will also explore real-world examples and case studies that demonstrate AI's impact on patient care.

Chapter 3: Machine Learning and Healthcare

Machine Learning (ML), a subset of Artificial Intelligence, has emerged as a powerful tool in the healthcare sector, transforming the way medical professionals diagnose and treat diseases. In this chapter, we will delve into the fundamentals of machine learning, explore its diverse applications in healthcare, and examine real-world case studies of successful ML applications in disease diagnosis.

Machine Learning Fundamentals

At its core, Machine Learning is a data-driven approach to problem-solving that enables computers to learn and make predictions or decisions without being explicitly programmed. It encompasses a variety of techniques and algorithms, each suited for different types of tasks. Here are some fundamental concepts and techniques within machine learning:

Supervised Learning: In supervised learning, an algorithm is trained on labeled data, where the outcome or target variable is known. The model learns to make predictions or classifications based on this training data. In healthcare, this approach is often used for tasks such as disease diagnosis, where historical patient data serves as the labeled dataset.

Unsupervised Learning: Unsupervised learning involves training a model on data without explicit labels. The algorithm identifies patterns, clusters, or relationships within the data. It is particularly useful in healthcare for tasks like patient segmentation and anomaly detection.

Deep Learning: Deep learning is a subset of machine learning that uses artificial neural networks with multiple layers. These deep neural networks are particularly effective for tasks that require understanding complex data, such as interpreting medical images or genetic sequences.

Feature Engineering: Feature engineering involves selecting and transforming relevant features (attributes or variables) from the data to improve the model's performance. In healthcare, this process may involve extracting meaningful features from patient data to enhance diagnostic accuracy.

Cross-Validation: Cross-validation is a technique used to assess a model's performance by splitting the dataset into training and testing sets multiple times. It helps evaluate the model's ability to generalize to new, unseen data, a critical aspect in healthcare where model accuracy is paramount.

Ensemble Methods: Ensemble methods combine multiple machine learning models to improve predictive accuracy and reduce overfitting. In healthcare, ensemble methods are used to enhance diagnostic models.

Applications of Machine Learning in Healthcare

Machine learning has a wide range of applications in healthcare, enhancing various aspects of patient care, research, and healthcare administration. Some notable applications include:

Disease Diagnosis and Risk Prediction: ML models can analyze patient data, including medical histories, lab results, and genetic information, to diagnose diseases, predict disease risks, and recommend personalized treatment plans.

Medical Imaging Interpretation: Machine learning is revolutionizing medical imaging interpretation. AI algorithms can analyze X-rays, MRIs, CT scans, and pathology slides, assisting radiologists and pathologists in detecting abnormalities and making more accurate diagnoses.

Drug Discovery and Development: ML accelerates drug discovery by predicting drug-drug interactions, identifying potential drug candidates, and optimizing clinical trial designs. It can significantly reduce the time and cost of bringing new medications to market.

Patient Monitoring and Remote Care: Remote patient monitoring with ML enables real-time tracking of patient health data, allowing healthcare providers to monitor patients with chronic conditions, detect anomalies, and provide timely interventions.

Healthcare Operations and Administrative Efficiency: ML streamlines administrative tasks, from appointment scheduling and billing to resource allocation and inventory management, reducing operational costs and improving efficiency.

Genomic Medicine: Machine learning is instrumental in analyzing genetic data to identify genetic variations associated with diseases, facilitating personalized treatment plans.

Case Studies of Successful ML in Diagnosis

Machine learning has demonstrated remarkable success in the field of disease diagnosis. Here are a few case studies showcasing the impact of ML in real-world healthcare settings:

Case Study 1: Early Detection of Diabetic Retinopathy

Diabetic retinopathy is a leading cause of blindness among diabetic patients. ML models have been developed to analyze retinal images and identify signs of diabetic retinopathy at an early stage. These models have proven highly accurate, allowing for timely interventions to prevent vision loss.

Case Study 2: Predicting Heart Disease Risk

Machine learning models have been trained on extensive cardiovascular data to predict an individual's risk of developing heart disease. These models consider various risk factors, including age, cholesterol levels, and lifestyle factors. Predictive models can identify individuals at high risk, enabling early intervention and lifestyle changes.

Case Study 3: Skin Cancer Diagnosis

Dermatologists use ML-powered image analysis to diagnose skin cancer. By examining photographs of skin lesions, these models can distinguish between benign and malignant growths with a high degree of accuracy, providing rapid and accurate diagnoses.

Case Study 4: Identifying Stroke from Brain Scans

Machine learning models can analyze brain scans to identify signs of a stroke. These models can detect lesions, blood clots, or other abnormalities that may not be immediately apparent to human radiologists, ensuring rapid treatment and improved patient outcomes.

Case Study 5: Detecting Alzheimer's Disease from Speech Patterns

ML algorithms can analyze speech patterns to detect early signs of Alzheimer's disease. These models can provide an early warning for cognitive decline, enabling timely interventions and support for affected individuals.

Chapter 4: Deep Learning and Medical Imaging

Deep Learning, a subfield of Machine Learning, has gained significant traction in healthcare, particularly in the domain of medical imaging. This chapter delves into the role of Deep Learning in healthcare, its impact on improving medical imaging, and the pivotal aspect of diagnostic accuracy when AI meets radiology.

Deep Learning in Healthcare

Deep Learning is a subset of machine learning that utilizes artificial neural networks with multiple layers to process and interpret complex data. Its ability to automatically discover intricate patterns within data makes it especially well-suited for healthcare applications, particularly in medical imaging interpretation.

The key elements of Deep Learning in healthcare include:

Convolutional Neural Networks (CNNs): CNNs are a fundamental architecture in Deep Learning, designed to analyze visual data. They have been transformative in image analysis, enabling the identification of features and patterns in medical images like X-rays, MRIs, and CT scans.

Transfer Learning: Transfer learning leverages pre-trained neural network models on large datasets and fine-tunes them for specific medical imaging tasks. This approach allows for effective use of limited medical image datasets.

Anomaly Detection: Deep Learning models excel in anomaly detection, making them invaluable for identifying abnormalities or deviations in medical images.

Natural Language Processing (NLP): Deep Learning also plays a role in interpreting and extracting insights from unstructured clinical notes and radiology reports, further enhancing diagnostic precision.

Improving Medical Imaging with Deep Learning

Deep Learning has significantly improved the field of medical imaging in several ways:

Enhanced Accuracy: Deep Learning models, particularly CNNs, have demonstrated exceptional accuracy in interpreting medical images. They can detect subtle abnormalities that may go unnoticed by human radiologists, improving diagnostic precision.

Faster Diagnosis: AI-powered medical imaging can provide rapid, automated initial assessments, expediting the diagnosis process and enabling timely interventions.

Standardization: Deep Learning models can help standardize the interpretation of medical images, reducing variations in diagnostic accuracy across different radiologists.

Large-Scale Screening: Deep Learning enables large-scale screening programs, particularly for diseases like cancer, where early detection is critical. Automated screening can process a high volume of images efficiently.

Quality Control: AI can assist in quality control by identifying errors or inconsistencies in medical images, ensuring that images meet the required standards.

Personalized Treatment Plans: Deep Learning can provide insights into treatment plans based on medical image analysis, tailoring interventions to individual patients.

Diagnostic Accuracy and AI

The diagnostic accuracy of AI in medical imaging is a pivotal aspect of its integration into healthcare. Deep Learning models are meticulously trained on vast datasets of medical images and are continuously fine-tuned to achieve higher levels of accuracy.

Sensitivity and Specificity: Deep Learning models aim to maximize both sensitivity and specificity. Sensitivity ensures that the model detects as many true positives as possible, minimizing false negatives. Specificity reduces false positives, ensuring that the model doesn't mistakenly identify healthy tissues as abnormal.

Training Data: The quality and quantity of training data are paramount. Deep Learning models require diverse and comprehensive datasets to learn from, representing a wide range of diseases, patient demographics, and imaging conditions.

Validation and Testing: To ensure diagnostic accuracy, AI models undergo rigorous validation and testing. Independent datasets are used to assess the model's performance and generalization ability. Regular evaluations are critical to monitor the model's ongoing accuracy.

Human Oversight: While AI can provide rapid and accurate initial assessments, human radiologists and healthcare professionals play a crucial role in interpreting and validating the AI's findings. AI is viewed as a tool to support, not replace, healthcare experts.

Ongoing Improvement: AI models continually improve their diagnostic accuracy through continuous learning. They can adapt to new insights and emerging medical knowledge, contributing to enhanced diagnostic precision over time.

In the chapters that follow, we will explore real-world examples of Deep Learning in medical imaging, including its applications in diagnosing a wide range of conditions from cancer to neurological disorders. These case studies will demonstrate the transformative power of Deep Learning in healthcare, particularly in the realm of medical imaging, where precision and speed are paramount.

Chapter 5: Natural Language Processing in Healthcare

Natural Language Processing (NLP) is a branch of Artificial Intelligence that focuses on the interaction between computers and human language. In healthcare, NLP plays a pivotal role in understanding, interpreting, and generating human language, enabling a more efficient exchange of medical information. This chapter explores the fundamentals of NLP, its applications in healthcare, including translating medical jargon, and its role in enhancing clinical documentation.

NLP Basics and Applications

NLP is built on a foundation of linguistic and computational principles, enabling it to analyze, understand, and generate human language. In healthcare, it offers a range of applications, such as:

Clinical Documentation: NLP simplifies the process of creating clinical notes, patient records, and reports by converting spoken language into written text. This application enhances the efficiency of healthcare professionals, allowing them to spend more time with patients and less on paperwork.

Medical Transcription: NLP systems can transcribe recorded conversations or dictations, making it easier to document patient visits, procedures, and other healthcare interactions.

Disease Coding: NLP automates the coding of medical conditions and treatments using standardized codes such as ICD-10. This ensures accurate billing and data for medical research.

Patient-Provider Interaction: NLP can assist in facilitating interactions between patients and healthcare providers through virtual assistants or chatbots. Patients can ask questions, receive health advice, and schedule appointments using natural language.

Semantic Search: NLP enables semantic search in electronic health records (EHRs) and medical literature. This functionality allows healthcare professionals to access relevant information more quickly.

Drug Information Retrieval: NLP helps in retrieving information about drugs, including their indications, dosages, and side effects, from vast medical databases.

Translating Medical Jargon

One of the key challenges in healthcare is the prevalence of medical jargon. Physicians and healthcare professionals often communicate using specialized terminology that can be difficult for the general population to understand. NLP bridges this gap by translating medical jargon into plain language:

Patient-Friendly Explanations: NLP algorithms can take complex medical terminology and translate it into patient-friendly explanations. This simplification helps patients better comprehend their conditions, treatments, and care plans.

Interoperability: In a healthcare ecosystem where different providers may use various terms, NLP can help standardize the language used across healthcare systems, improving interoperability and data sharing.

Multilingual Communication: NLP is also instrumental in enabling multilingual communication, ensuring that patients from diverse linguistic backgrounds can access healthcare information in their preferred languages.

Provider-Patient Communication: NLP facilitates clear communication between healthcare providers and patients, ensuring that the patient fully grasps their diagnosis, treatment options, and care plan.

Medical Literature Access: NLP can assist in understanding complex medical literature and research papers, making the latest medical findings more accessible to healthcare professionals and researchers.

Enhancing Clinical Documentation

Clinical documentation is a critical aspect of healthcare, as it is essential for accurate diagnosis, treatment, and medical research. NLP enhances clinical documentation in several ways:

Efficiency: NLP streamlines the clinical documentation process by automatically transcribing spoken words, allowing healthcare professionals to focus more on patient care and less on manual data entry.

Accuracy: NLP can reduce errors in documentation by interpreting spoken language accurately, ensuring that the patient's medical history and care plan are recorded with precision.

Structured Data Entry: NLP can extract structured data from clinical notes, converting unstructured text into standardized data that can be used for analytics, research, and billing.

Voice Recognition: NLP-based voice recognition systems allow healthcare professionals to dictate clinical notes and reports, which are then transcribed with high accuracy.

Suggested Diagnoses and Treatments: NLP systems can provide healthcare professionals with suggested diagnoses and treatment options based on the information provided, reducing the cognitive load during patient visits.

Quality Control: NLP can assist in quality control, identifying inconsistencies or missing information in clinical notes, ensuring that the documentation meets regulatory and quality standards.

In the chapters that follow, we will explore real-world applications of NLP in healthcare, including case studies where NLP has transformed the way healthcare professionals communicate, document patient interactions, and provide clear and understandable information to patients. The power of NLP in healthcare lies in its ability to bridge the language gap and streamline clinical documentation, ultimately leading to more effective patient care and improved healthcare outcomes.

Chapter 6: AI in Disease Diagnosis

Artificial Intelligence (AI) has emerged as a transformative force in healthcare, particularly in the domain of disease diagnosis. This chapter explores the application of AI in the early detection of diseases, the development of AI-enabled diagnostic tools, and its role in reducing misdiagnoses—a critical aspect of improving patient outcomes.

Early Detection of Diseases

The early detection of diseases is a crucial factor in the effectiveness of medical treatment. Detecting diseases in their early stages can significantly improve patient outcomes, increase the chances of successful treatment, and reduce healthcare costs. AI plays a pivotal role in early disease detection through several methods:

Analysis of Medical Imaging: AI algorithms are trained to analyze medical images, such as X-rays, MRIs, CT scans, and pathology slides, to detect subtle signs of diseases. For example, in the case of cancer, AI can identify small tumors or anomalies that may be challenging for human radiologists to notice at an early stage.

Genomic Analysis: AI assists in analyzing genomic data to identify genetic variations associated with hereditary diseases, cancer risk, and other conditions. Early identification of such genetic markers allows for preventive measures and early interventions.

Remote Monitoring: AI-powered wearable devices and remote monitoring systems continuously track patients' health parameters. Sudden deviations from normal readings can trigger alerts, enabling early diagnosis and interventions for conditions like cardiac arrhythmias or diabetes-related complications.

Predictive Analytics: AI can predict the risk of developing specific diseases by analyzing a patient's medical history, genetics, lifestyle, and environmental factors. This allows for preventive measures and regular screenings to detect diseases in their early stages.

Symptom Analysis: Chatbots and virtual assistants powered by AI can engage with patients to understand their symptoms and medical history, helping in the early identification of diseases.

Big Data Analysis: AI can analyze vast sets of patient data to identify patterns and trends related to disease development. This data-driven approach allows for the early identification of emerging diseases or outbreaks.

AI-Enabled Diagnostic Tools

AI-enabled diagnostic tools have revolutionized the healthcare landscape by providing accurate and rapid disease diagnosis. These tools are transforming the way healthcare professionals operate, leading to more efficient and precise diagnosis and treatment. Some notable AI-enabled diagnostic tools include:

Computer-Aided Diagnosis (CAD) Systems: CAD systems assist radiologists in interpreting medical images. They can detect abnormalities in X-rays, mammograms, and other imaging studies, significantly improving diagnostic accuracy.

Pathology AI: Pathology AI assists pathologists in diagnosing diseases by analyzing tissue samples. It can detect abnormalities, classify cancer types, and estimate disease progression, contributing to more precise treatment plans.

Disease-Specific AI Models: AI models are developed for specific diseases, such as diabetic retinopathy, skin cancer, and lung diseases. These models can diagnose these conditions with high accuracy, ensuring early detection and intervention.

Genomic AI Analysis: AI tools analyze genomic data to identify genetic variations associated with diseases, providing insights into disease risk and potential preventive measures.

Diagnostic Chatbots: AI-powered chatbots engage with patients to collect symptom and medical history data, offering preliminary disease diagnoses and guidance on seeking medical attention.

Point-of-Care Testing: AI-powered diagnostic devices are increasingly being used at the point of care. These devices can rapidly analyze blood samples, urine, or other specimens, providing quick diagnostic results.

Telemedicine Platforms: AI is integrated into telemedicine platforms, enabling remote consultations and diagnostic services. Patients can receive preliminary diagnoses and recommendations without leaving their homes.

Reducing Misdiagnoses with AI

Misdiagnoses in healthcare can lead to severe consequences, including delayed treatment, unnecessary procedures, and patient harm. AI has demonstrated significant potential in reducing misdiagnoses by providing healthcare professionals with accurate and data-driven insights:

Consistency: AI algorithms consistently analyze medical images and data, eliminating variability in interpretation that may occur among human healthcare professionals. This consistency improves diagnostic accuracy.

Speed: AI processes medical data and images at incredible speeds, providing rapid results to healthcare professionals. Quick diagnoses can be critical in cases where timely treatment is essential.

Pattern Recognition: AI excels in recognizing patterns and anomalies. It can identify subtle signs of diseases that may be challenging for human healthcare professionals to detect.

Data Integration: AI can integrate data from various sources, such as medical records, imaging, and genetic information. This comprehensive approach provides a more holistic view of a patient's health, reducing the likelihood of misdiagnoses.

Quality Control: AI can help ensure the quality of clinical documentation and imaging, reducing errors that may lead to misdiagnoses.

Decision Support: AI-powered decision support systems offer recommendations to healthcare professionals, ensuring that diagnoses are based on the latest medical knowledge and guidelines.

Second Opinions: AI can provide a second opinion to healthcare professionals, confirming or challenging initial diagnoses to reduce the risk of misdiagnoses.

As we explore the real-world applications of AI in disease diagnosis in the chapters that follow, we will discover how AI has transformed the healthcare landscape by enabling early disease detection, enhancing diagnostic tools, and minimizing the occurrence of misdiagnoses.

CHAPTER 7: PERSONALIZED

TREATMENT PLANS WITH AI

Personalized treatment plans in healthcare have gained prominence as a means to deliver tailored medical care that considers an individual's unique characteristics and medical history. Artificial Intelligence (AI) has played a pivotal role in the development of personalized treatment plans. This chapter explores how AI tailors treatment options, aids in medication selection, and employs predictive analytics to optimize patient outcomes.

Tailoring Treatment Options

Personalized treatment plans involve customizing medical care to suit the specific needs and conditions of each patient. AI contributes to the tailoring of treatment options in various ways:

Patient Data Analysis: AI analyzes a patient's medical history, genetic data, lifestyle, and environmental factors to gain a comprehensive understanding of their health. This data-driven approach ensures that treatment options are tailored to the individual's unique situation.

Precision Medicine: Precision medicine, which leverages genetic and molecular information, is a significant component of personalized treatment. AI helps identify genetic markers associated with diseases, allowing for targeted therapies that have a higher likelihood of success.

Treatment Recommendations: AI provides healthcare professionals with data-driven treatment recommendations based on the latest medical research, guidelines, and clinical evidence. These recommendations take into account the patient's specific conditions and preferences.

Optimizing Therapeutic Strategies: AI algorithms continuously analyze patient responses to treatment, enabling adjustments and optimization of therapeutic strategies. This dynamic approach ensures that treatments are effective and well-tolerated.

Personalized Cancer Therapy: In cancer treatment, AI helps identify specific tumor characteristics and genetic mutations, allowing oncologists to select treatments that target the cancer's vulnerabilities while minimizing harm to healthy tissues.

Psychological and Behavioral Interventions: AI can assess a patient's psychological and behavioral factors and recommend appropriate interventions. For example, AI can suggest therapy approaches for mental health conditions, ensuring that the treatment plan aligns with the patient's needs.

Preventive Measures: AI assists in identifying individuals at high risk for specific conditions and provides recommendations for preventive measures, such as lifestyle changes, screening, or vaccination.

AI in Medication Selection

Medication selection is a critical aspect of healthcare, and AI is playing an increasing role in ensuring that patients receive the most suitable and effective drugs. AI's impact on medication selection includes:

Pharmacogenomics: AI analyzes genetic data to identify how a patient's genes may affect their response to specific medications. This enables healthcare professionals to prescribe drugs that are most likely to be effective and have minimal side effects.

Drug-Drug Interaction Predictions: AI algorithms assess potential interactions between medications to avoid adverse effects. This is particularly important for patients with multiple prescriptions.

Medication Efficacy Predictions: AI can predict how effective a medication is likely to be for a specific patient's condition. This allows healthcare professionals to select drugs with the highest probability of success.

Personalized Dosage: AI can determine the optimal dosage of medications based on a patient's unique characteristics, ensuring that the medication achieves the desired therapeutic effect.

Medication Adherence: AI-powered tools can monitor patient adherence to prescribed medications and provide reminders and interventions to improve compliance.

Allergy and Sensitivity Analysis: AI helps identify patient allergies and sensitivities, ensuring that medications do not trigger adverse reactions.

Adverse Event Monitoring: AI continually monitors patient data for potential adverse events related to medications, allowing for early intervention if issues arise.

Predictive Analytics for Patient Outcomes

AI-driven predictive analytics is a cornerstone of personalized treatment planning. By assessing historical patient data, treatment responses, and various influencing factors, AI can predict patient outcomes:

Disease Progression: AI can predict how a disease is likely to progress in a specific patient. This information guides healthcare professionals in adjusting treatment plans as needed.

Treatment Response: Predictive analytics assess the patient's likely response to a treatment, ensuring that the chosen therapy is appropriate and effective.

Hospital Readmission Risk: AI can estimate the risk of hospital readmission, enabling healthcare professionals to provide additional support to high-risk patients.

Survival Rates: AI models can predict survival rates for patients with certain conditions, helping healthcare professionals and patients make informed decisions about treatment options.

Outcome Optimization: AI continually optimizes treatment plans to ensure that patients receive the most effective care and achieve the best possible outcomes.

Resource Allocation: Predictive analytics can assist healthcare organizations in allocating resources more efficiently by anticipating patient needs and trends in healthcare demand.

The chapters that follow will explore real-world applications of AI in personalized treatment planning. We will delve into case studies that demonstrate how AI is revolutionizing the way healthcare professionals customize treatment options, enhance medication selection, and optimize patient outcomes, ultimately leading to more effective and patient-centric healthcare delivery.

Chapter 8: Robotics and Automation in Healthcare

Robotics and automation have ushered in a new era of healthcare, transforming medical practices and enhancing patient care. This chapter delves into the use of surgical robots and artificial intelligence, the automation of hospital operations, and the application of robotics in rehabilitation and patient care.

Surgical Robots and AI

Minimally Invasive Surgery: Surgical robots, often guided by AI, have revolutionized minimally invasive surgery. These robots provide enhanced precision and dexterity, enabling surgeons to perform complex procedures through tiny incisions. For example, the da Vinci Surgical System has become a mainstay in various surgical disciplines, from urology to gynecology.

Enhanced Visualization: Surgical robots offer 3D visualization, allowing surgeons to see intricate anatomical structures with unparalleled clarity. This aids in precise dissection and tissue sparing during surgery.

Robot-Assisted Procedures: AI-powered robots assist surgeons in performing procedures with great precision. The collaboration between the surgeon and the robot enhances the overall safety and efficacy of the surgery.

Telesurgery: Robotics, combined with AI, enable telesurgery, where a surgeon can perform a procedure from a remote location. This has implications for reaching patients in remote areas and during emergency situations.

Reduced Invasiveness: AI and robotics enable procedures that are less invasive, reducing the patient's postoperative pain, scarring, and recovery time. This is particularly important in fields like cardiac surgery and orthopedics.

Training and Skill Enhancement: Surgical robots with AI can serve as training tools for surgeons, allowing them to refine their skills in a controlled environment before performing actual surgeries. This reduces the learning curve and enhances the quality of healthcare.

Hospital Automation and Efficiency

Administrative Tasks: Automation is employed in managing administrative tasks, such as appointment scheduling, billing, and record-keeping. AI-driven chatbots handle patient inquiries, appointment scheduling, and administrative support.

Patient Records and Data: Electronic Health Records (EHRs) have revolutionized healthcare data management. Automation ensures the efficient storage, retrieval, and secure sharing of patient records among healthcare providers.

Supply Chain Management: Hospitals employ robotics and AI for managing their supply chains. Automated systems track inventory levels, order supplies as needed, and reduce waste. This ensures that critical medical supplies are always available.

Pharmacy Automation: Robots and AI assist pharmacists by dispensing medications, verifying prescriptions, and packaging drugs. This reduces errors and improves efficiency in medication management.

Patient Flow: Automation optimizes patient flow within hospitals, reducing waiting times and improving the overall patient experience. This is particularly important in emergency departments and outpatient clinics.

Patient Monitoring: Automation in patient monitoring includes wearable devices and remote monitoring systems. These technologies continuously track patient health and can alert healthcare providers to potential issues, facilitating early interventions.

Robotic Rehabilitation and Patient Care

Rehabilitation Robots: Robotics plays a crucial role in physical therapy and rehabilitation. Robots assist patients in regaining mobility, strength, and coordination after injuries or surgeries. Exoskeletons, for example, enable patients with spinal cord injuries to walk again.

Assistive Devices: Robotic devices provide assistance to individuals with disabilities or limitations. Prosthetic limbs, powered wheelchairs, and other assistive technologies enhance the independence and quality of life of patients with physical impairments.

Mental Health Support: AI-driven chatbots and virtual assistants offer mental health support, providing patients with resources and assistance for managing stress, anxiety, and other mental health challenges.

Patient Engagement: Robots and AI-driven patient engagement tools help individuals manage their health and wellness. These systems provide reminders for medication, exercise, and dietary restrictions, empowering patients to take an active role in their healthcare.

Telemedicine and Telehealth: The combination of robotics and telemedicine allows patients to receive medical consultations and therapy remotely. Robotic devices, controlled by healthcare professionals, can provide diagnostic assessments and guidance to patients from a distance.

Elderly Care: Robotics assists in elderly care by providing companionship, assisting with daily tasks, and monitoring the health and well-being of elderly individuals. These robotic caregivers offer support to the aging population.

Pediatric Care: Robots, with their engaging and non-threatening designs, assist in pediatric care. They can serve as tools for distraction and play during medical procedures, making the healthcare experience less stressful for children.

The chapters that follow will explore real-world applications of robotics and automation in healthcare, including case studies that demonstrate how these technologies are revolutionizing surgical procedures, streamlining hospital operations, and enhancing patient care. Robotics and automation have brought about transformative changes in the healthcare sector, and their impact on patient outcomes and healthcare efficiency continues to grow.

Chapter 9: Remote Patient Monitoring

Remote patient monitoring (RPM) is a revolutionary approach to healthcare that utilizes technology to monitor patients outside traditional clinical settings. This chapter delves into the role of the Internet of Things (IoT) in remote monitoring, the influence of artificial intelligence in patient management, and strategies to enhance patient engagement in remote care.

The Role of IoT in Remote Monitoring

Connected Devices: The IoT ecosystem encompasses a wide array of connected medical devices, wearables, and sensors that collect patient data.

These devices include blood pressure monitors, glucose meters, ECG patches, and more. Patients use these devices to track their health parameters, and the data is sent to healthcare providers for real-time monitoring.

Continuous Data Streams: IoT-enabled devices provide continuous data streams, offering a comprehensive view of a patient's health. This is particularly valuable for individuals with chronic conditions such as diabetes, hypertension, or heart disease. Continuous monitoring helps healthcare providers identify trends and intervene promptly.

Wireless Connectivity: IoT devices communicate wirelessly, ensuring that patients can transmit their data without the need for physical connections. This convenience promotes patient adherence and reduces barriers to remote monitoring.

Real-Time Alerts: IoT devices can trigger real-time alerts to both patients and healthcare providers. For instance, if a patient's blood glucose level becomes dangerously low, the system can send an alert to the patient and their care team, enabling swift action.

Geolocation Services: IoT can also include geolocation services, allowing healthcare providers to track the whereabouts of patients. This is useful for monitoring the movements of patients with dementia or cognitive impairments.

Data Analytics: The vast amounts of data collected through IoT devices are analyzed using AI and data analytics. Patterns and anomalies in the data are identified, helping healthcare providers make informed decisions about patient care.

AI-Driven Remote Patient Management

Data Analysis: Artificial intelligence processes and interprets the data collected from remote monitoring devices. AI algorithms can identify significant changes in a patient's health metrics, such as sudden blood pressure spikes or irregular heart rhythms. These changes trigger alerts for timely intervention.

Risk Stratification: AI employs predictive analytics to stratify patients by risk. Patients at higher risk of complications or hospitalization can receive more focused attention and resources.

Personalized Care Plans: AI tailors care plans to each patient's unique needs. It can suggest medication adjustments, dietary changes, or exercise routines based on individual health data.

Medication Management: AI systems help manage medication adherence by sending reminders and providing educational resources. Patients are less likely to forget to take their medications when supported by AI-driven medication management tools.

Chatbots and Virtual Assistants: AI-powered chatbots and virtual assistants are used to engage with patients, answer their healthcare queries, and offer guidance. These systems provide valuable information and improve patient engagement.

Telehealth Integration: AI facilitates telehealth consultations by analyzing patient data and providing real-time insights to healthcare providers during remote visits. This ensures that telehealth consultations are as informative and effective as in-person visits.

Population Health Management: AI supports population health management by analyzing data from a group of patients. It identifies trends, potential outbreaks, or common health issues that can inform public health efforts and resource allocation.

Improving Patient Engagement

Patient Education: Effective patient engagement begins with education. Healthcare providers offer resources and information to patients, ensuring they understand their conditions, treatment plans, and the importance of remote monitoring.

Interactive Platforms: Patients have access to interactive platforms where they can view their health data, ask questions, and track their progress. Gamified elements, progress bars, and rewards can enhance engagement.

Regular Communication: Healthcare providers maintain regular communication with patients through messages, phone calls, or virtual visits. This ensures that patients feel supported and can address any concerns promptly.

Feedback and Goal Setting: Patients set goals for their health, and healthcare providers offer feedback and encouragement to help them achieve these objectives. Achieving milestones promotes patient engagement.

Patient Empowerment: Empowering patients to take an active role in their healthcare promotes engagement. Patients can make decisions about their care and feel more in control of their health outcomes.

Support Networks: Patients are encouraged to involve their support networks, including family and friends, in their healthcare journey. This social support enhances engagement and provides a network for patients to turn to in times of need.

Remote Health Communities: Online communities and forums offer a space for patients to connect with others facing similar health challenges. These communities provide emotional support and shared experiences, fostering engagement.

In the chapters that follow, we will explore real-world applications of remote patient monitoring, highlighting how IoT devices, AI-driven patient management, and effective patient engagement strategies are transforming healthcare. Remote monitoring has the potential to enhance patient outcomes, reduce healthcare costs, and increase the accessibility of medical care, ultimately improving the quality of healthcare delivery.

Chapter 10: AI in Drug Discovery

AI has emerged as a game-changer in the field of drug discovery and development. This chapter delves into the ways AI accelerates drug development, enables targeted therapies, and showcases successful case studies of AI-driven drug discoveries.

Accelerating Drug Development

Data Analysis: AI processes vast amounts of biomedical data, from genetic information to clinical trial results. By analyzing this data, AI identifies potential drug targets, biomarkers, and disease pathways.

Drug Repurposing: AI can identify existing drugs with potential new applications, a process known as drug repurposing. By analyzing existing data, AI uncovers opportunities to use approved drugs to treat other diseases.

Virtual Screening: AI streamlines the drug discovery process through virtual screening, which simulates the interaction between potential drug compounds and biological targets. This saves time and resources by identifying promising drug candidates before physical testing.

AI-Driven Research: AI-powered laboratory robots conduct experiments and tests, reducing the need for manual labor and accelerating research timelines. These robots can run high-throughput screenings, analyze results, and refine experiments autonomously.

Clinical Trial Optimization: AI identifies eligible patient populations and optimizes the design of clinical trials. By selecting the right participants and designing efficient trials, AI accelerates the evaluation of new drugs.

Drug Design: AI assists in designing new drug compounds. It predicts the chemical structures of potential drugs, which can then be synthesized and tested.

Targeted Therapies with AI

Personalized Medicine: AI tailors treatments to individual patients based on their genetic makeup, biomarkers, and response to therapy. This leads to more effective and precise treatments with fewer side effects.

Biomarker Discovery: AI identifies biomarkers that indicate the likelihood of disease, disease progression, or treatment response. These biomarkers help determine the most appropriate therapies for patients.

Genomic Profiling: AI analyzes genomic data to uncover genetic mutations and variations that can be targeted with specific drugs. Genomic profiling informs the development of therapies that address the unique characteristics of each patient's disease.

Immunotherapy Enhancement: AI supports the development of immunotherapies by identifying cancer antigens and predicting how the immune system will respond to specific treatments. This enables the design of effective immunotherapies for cancer patients.

Drug Combination Identification: AI identifies optimal combinations of drugs to enhance therapeutic outcomes. These combinations may target multiple disease pathways simultaneously, increasing treatment efficacy.

Adaptive Therapies: AI continuously monitors patients and adjusts treatments in real-time based on their changing health status. This approach maximizes treatment effectiveness and minimizes side effects.

Case Studies of Successful Drug Discoveries

Insilico Medicine: Insilico Medicine is a company that has used AI to discover potential drug candidates for a range of diseases, including cancer, fibrosis, and Parkinson's disease. The company's AI algorithms analyze vast datasets to identify promising drug compounds quickly.

Atomwise: Atomwise leverages AI for drug discovery by virtually screening millions of compounds to identify potential drug candidates. The company's AI technology has led to the discovery of treatments for conditions like Ebola and multiple sclerosis.

DeepMind: DeepMind, a subsidiary of Alphabet, has used AI to predict the 3D structures of proteins. This breakthrough has significant implications for drug discovery, as understanding protein structures helps identify potential drug targets.

BenevolentAI: BenevolentAI uses AI to analyze biomedical data and identify potential drug targets. The company's AI platform has contributed to the discovery of new drug candidates for diseases like amyotrophic lateral sclerosis (ALS) and Parkinson's disease.

Recursion Pharmaceuticals: Recursion Pharmaceuticals applies AI to repurpose existing drugs for new indications. By systematically testing known drugs on various diseases, the company has identified potential treatments for diseases such as cerebral cavernous malformations.

AI-Driven Vaccine Discovery: AI has played a critical role in accelerating vaccine development. During the COVID-19 pandemic, AI helped identify potential vaccine candidates, shortening the development timeline and enabling a rapid response to the global health crisis.

AI's impact on drug discovery is transforming the pharmaceutical industry, making the process more efficient and effective. As AI continues to evolve and integrate into drug development pipelines, it holds the promise of bringing novel therapies to market faster and tailoring treatments to individual patients' needs, ultimately improving healthcare outcomes. In the chapters that follow, we will delve into the real-world applications of AI in drug discovery, highlighting the breakthroughs and innovations that are reshaping the field.

Chapter 11: Ethical and Legal Considerations

The integration of artificial intelligence (AI) in healthcare introduces a myriad of ethical and legal considerations. This chapter explores the challenges and issues related to patient privacy and data security, AI liability, malpractice, and the regulatory frameworks that govern AI in healthcare.

Patient Privacy and Data Security

Data Protection: As healthcare providers and institutions collect and store vast amounts of patient data, safeguarding this information is paramount. AI systems require access to sensitive patient information, raising concerns about data breaches and privacy violations.

Informed Consent: Patients must be adequately informed about how their data will be used in AI-driven healthcare applications. Obtaining informed consent ensures that patients are aware of the potential uses of their data and can make choices about its sharing and usage.

Data Anonymization: AI developers should implement data anonymization techniques to protect patient identities. This process removes personally identifiable information while retaining the utility of data for AI applications.

Secure Data Transfer: Data transferred between healthcare institutions, AI systems, and researchers must be encrypted and secure. Ensuring that data is not intercepted or tampered with during transmission is critical for maintaining patient privacy.

Access Controls: Healthcare organizations should implement strict access controls to restrict data access to authorized personnel only. This helps prevent unauthorized access to patient records and AI models.

Data Retention Policies: Establishing clear data retention policies ensures that patient data is not stored longer than necessary, minimizing the risk of data breaches.

AI Liability and Malpractice

Algorithmic Accountability: As AI systems make autonomous decisions in patient care, questions arise about who is responsible when these systems make errors. Healthcare providers, developers, and regulatory bodies must consider the concept of algorithmic accountability to determine liability.

Malpractice Concerns: In the event of AI-related errors, determining malpractice liability is complex. Was the AI system properly maintained and updated? Did the healthcare provider exercise due diligence in using the AI system? These questions must be addressed.

Transparency and Interpretability: The opacity of some AI algorithms can lead to difficulties in understanding how a decision was made. This lack of transparency may affect malpractice cases, as it may be challenging to assess whether an AI system acted in a manner consistent with medical standards.

Human Oversight: AI in healthcare often operates with human oversight. Healthcare providers must balance their reliance on AI with their own judgment and responsibilities. Determining when and how to override AI decisions is crucial.

Regulatory Compliance: AI systems must adhere to regulatory requirements, including those related to patient safety and medical standards. Failure to comply with these regulations may result in legal liability.

Regulatory Frameworks

FDA Oversight: The U.S. Food and Drug Administration (FDA) plays a critical role in regulating medical devices, including AI applications. Developers of AI systems must navigate the FDA's approval processes, ensuring that their products meet safety and efficacy standards.

HIPAA Compliance: The Health Insurance Portability and Accountability Act (HIPAA) in the United States imposes strict requirements on the privacy and security of patient health information. AI systems in healthcare must comply with HIPAA regulations to protect patient data.

GDPR in Europe: The General Data Protection Regulation (GDPR) in the European Union sets stringent rules for the processing of personal data, including healthcare data. AI systems used in Europe must adhere to GDPR principles to ensure patient data privacy.

Ethical Guidelines: Healthcare organizations often establish ethical guidelines for the use of AI in patient care. These guidelines define best practices and standards for AI implementation, emphasizing transparency, fairness, and ethical considerations.

International Harmonization: The international harmonization of AI regulations is an ongoing effort. International organizations and collaborations work to create unified standards and frameworks for AI in healthcare to ensure global consistency.

Transparency and Accountability: Regulatory frameworks increasingly require transparency and accountability in AI systems. Developers must document the development process, provide explanations for AI decisions, and ensure traceability.

The ethical and legal considerations surrounding AI in healthcare are evolving as technology advances and becomes more integrated into medical practice. Healthcare organizations, regulatory bodies, and AI developers must collaborate to address these concerns, ensuring that AI applications in healthcare prioritize patient privacy, safety, and adherence to legal standards. The chapters that follow will further explore the ethical and legal dimensions of AI in healthcare, offering insights into the evolving landscape of ethical and legal considerations in this dynamic field.

Chapter 12: Future of AI in Healthcare

The future of artificial intelligence (AI) in healthcare is a promising landscape filled with emerging trends, cutting-edge technologies, and transformative possibilities. In this chapter, we explore these developments, make predictions about the future of healthcare, and discuss preparations for the next generation of healthcare AI.

Emerging Trends and Technologies

AI in Drug Discovery: AI's role in drug discovery is poised to grow significantly. Advanced AI algorithms will expedite drug development, leading to a higher number of effective treatments for a wide range of diseases.

Personalized Medicine: The future of healthcare will focus on personalized medicine, driven by AI. Treatment plans will be tailored to each patient's unique genetic makeup, biomarkers, and lifestyle factors, resulting in more effective therapies with fewer side effects.

AI-Enhanced Imaging: AI will continue to revolutionize medical imaging. Radiologists and clinicians will benefit from AI algorithms that can detect and diagnose a variety of medical conditions from images with exceptional accuracy.

AI in Genomic Medicine: Genomic medicine, a field that examines an individual's genetic code to inform medical decisions, will be increasingly shaped by AI. AI will analyze complex genomic data to predict disease risk, customize treatments, and improve patient outcomes.

Remote Monitoring and Telehealth: AI-powered remote monitoring devices will become more prevalent, allowing healthcare providers to track patient health in real-time. Telehealth will continue to expand, offering convenient and accessible healthcare services.

Healthcare Chatbots and Virtual Health Assistants: AI-driven healthcare chatbots and virtual health assistants will play a prominent role in patient engagement and health management. They will provide information, answer questions, and offer guidance on various healthcare topics.

AI-Enabled Robotics: Robotics will be enhanced by AI, contributing to more advanced surgical procedures, better patient care, and efficient hospital operations. Surgical robots, rehabilitation devices, and assistive robots will become more integrated into healthcare settings.

AI for Predictive Analytics: AI will power predictive analytics models that can forecast disease outbreaks, patient admission rates, and resource needs for healthcare facilities. This capability will help healthcare systems prepare for surges in demand and allocate resources effectively.

AI-Driven Behavioral Health: AI will play an essential role in behavioral health by analyzing patient data to detect early signs of mental health issues and provide personalized support. AI-based apps and platforms will offer mental health interventions and therapy.

Predictions for the Future of Healthcare

Early Disease Detection: AI will enable early detection of diseases, allowing for intervention before symptoms become severe. This will lead to better treatment outcomes and reduced healthcare costs.

AI-Enhanced Care Coordination: AI will improve care coordination among healthcare providers, leading to more efficient and seamless patient care. AI will assist in sharing medical records, appointments, and treatment plans.

Healthcare at Home: The use of AI and remote monitoring will enable more healthcare services to be provided at home. Patients will receive personalized care in the comfort of their own environment.

Preventive and Lifestyle Medicine: AI will promote preventive medicine and lifestyle interventions. AI-powered apps and wearables will provide real-time insights into patients' health, encouraging healthier habits and reducing the risk of chronic diseases.

Global Healthcare Access: Telehealth and AI-driven healthcare solutions will expand access to medical care, including in remote and underserved regions. This will address healthcare disparities and improve global healthcare equity.

AI in Medical Education: Medical education will increasingly incorporate AI-driven simulations, virtual reality, and AI tutors to enhance training and provide students with hands-on experiences.

Preparing for the Next Generation of Healthcare AI

Education and Training: Healthcare professionals need to receive education and training in AI to effectively leverage these technologies. Continuous learning will be crucial to stay updated with the latest AI applications.

Data Security and Privacy: Protecting patient data remains a top priority. Healthcare organizations must invest in robust cybersecurity measures and adhere to data privacy regulations.

Ethical Guidelines: Ethical considerations in AI healthcare applications are vital. The development and use of AI in healthcare must adhere to strict ethical guidelines to ensure patient trust and safety.

Regulatory Adaptation: Regulatory bodies must adapt to the evolving landscape of AI in healthcare. They should establish clear guidelines for AI-driven medical devices, data privacy, and ethical standards.

Research and Innovation: Continued research and innovation are essential for the future of healthcare AI. Collaboration between healthcare institutions, AI developers, and research organizations will drive advancements in the field.

Patient-Centric Approaches: Healthcare should adopt patient-centric approaches with AI. The patient's voice and choices should guide the development and implementation of AI technologies in healthcare.

Collaboration and Partnerships: Collaboration between healthcare providers, technology companies, research institutions, and regulatory agencies will foster a cohesive ecosystem for AI in healthcare.

Accessibility and Equity: Efforts must be made to ensure that AI-driven healthcare solutions are accessible to all, reducing healthcare disparities and promoting equitable care.

The future of AI in healthcare promises innovative solutions, enhanced patient care, and better healthcare outcomes. While exciting opportunities lie ahead, addressing ethical, regulatory, and data security concerns will be essential to realizing the full potential of AI in healthcare. Preparing for the next generation of healthcare AI requires a commitment to education, ethics, innovation, and patient-centered care.

Milton Keynes UK
Ingram Content Group UK Ltd.
UKHW022202030324
438776UK00012B/1874

9 798868 989216